THE BLACK DEATH AND THE PEASANTS' REVOLT

Tony D. Triggs

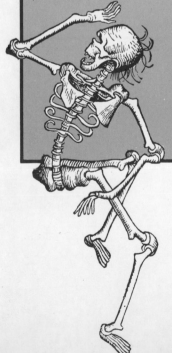

M
Macmillan Education

First published 1985
Reprinted 1986

Published by
MACMILLAN EDUCATION LTD
Houndmills, Basingstoke, Hampshire RG21 2XS
and London
Companies and representatives
throughout the world

Printed in Hong Kong

British Library Cataloguing in Publication Data
Triggs, Tony D.
The Black Death and the Peasants' Revolt.
—(History in depth)
1. Great Britain—History—Edward I–III,
1272-1377
I. Title   II. Series
942.03   DA225
ISBN 0–333–36851–7

CONTENTS

Acknowledgements

The author and publishers wish to acknowledge the following photograph sources:

British Library pp 24 top, 42, 44, 46;   Cambridge University Collection p 24 bottom;   A.F. Kersting p 23; Mansell Collection pp 17, 18, 21, 31 left, 38;   National Portrait Gallery, London p 31 right;   Rijksmuseum, Utrecht p 9.

The publishers have made every effort to trace the copyright holders, but where they have failed to do so they will be pleased to make the necessary arrangements at the first opportunity.

The author and publishers wish to thank K.R. Triggs for the translation of the Report by Sheriffs and Jurors of London, pp 39–40.

PREFACE

The study of history is exciting, whether in a good story well told, a mystery solved by the judicious unravelling of clues, or a study of the men, women and children whose fears and ambitions, successes and tragedies make up the collective memory of mankind.

This series aims to reveal this excitement to pupils through a set of topic books on important historical subjects from the Middle Ages to the present day. Each book contains four main elements: a narrative and descriptive text, lively and relevant illustrations, extracts of contemporary evidence, and questions for further thought and work. Involvement in these elements should provide an adventure which will bring the past to life in the imagination of the pupil.

Each book is also designed to develop the knowledge, skills and concepts so essential to a pupil's growth. It provides a wide, varying introduction to the evidence available on each topic. In handling this evidence, pupils will increase their understanding of basic historical concepts such as causation and change, as well as of more advanced ideas such as revolution and democracy. In addition, their use of basic study skills will be complemented by more sophisticated historical skills such as the detection of bias and the formulation of opinion.

The intended audience for the series is pupils of eleven to sixteen years: it is expected that the earlier topics will be introduced in the first three years of secondary school, while the nineteenth and twentieth century topics are directed towards first examinations.

THE PLAGUE REACHES EUROPE

Horrors and tempests

In the early part of the fourteenth century people in Europe began to hear of strange and terrible happenings in far-off lands. News of these things was brought by travellers. The following reports were written down by those who had listened to such accounts:

tempests: storms

A *In the East, in a certain province near where India extends to the north, horrors and unheard-of tempests overwhelmed the whole province for the space of three days. On the first day there was a rain of frogs, serpents, lizards, scorpions, and many venomous beasts of that sort. On the second, thunder was heard, and lightning and sheets of fire fell upon the earth, mingled with hail-stones of marvellous size; which slew almost all, from the greatest even to the least. On the third day there fell fire from heaven and stinking smoke, which slew all that were left of men and beasts, and burned up all the cities and towns in those parts.*

By these tempests the whole province was infected; and it is thought that through the foul blast of wind that came from the South, the whole seashore and surrounding lands were infected, and are growing more and more poisonous from day to day.

De Smet: *Recueil des Chroniques de Flandres*, vol. 3

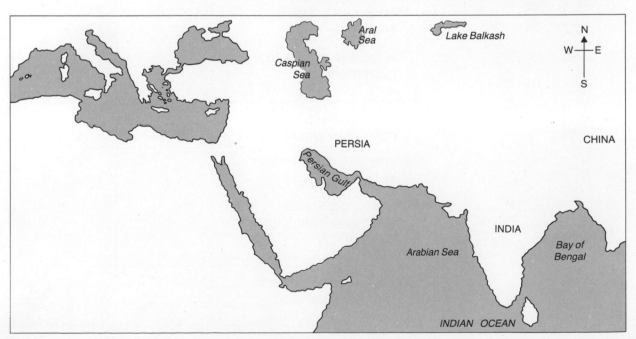

B *Between China and Persia [Iran] there rained a vast rain of fire, falling in flakes like snow and burning up mountains and plains and other lands, with men and women. And then arose vast masses of smoke, and whosoever beheld this died within the space of half a day, and likewise any man or woman who looked upon those who had seen this.*

Chronicon Estense, Muratori 3

Using the evidence: horror stories from the East

1   Look at the table. Beside each piece of information put a tick to show which report it is from. Put a tick in both columns if both reports say the same thing.

Information	Report A	Report B
Poisonous animals fall from the sky		
There is thunder and lightning		
Fire falls to earth		
The fire is mixed with giant hailstones		
The fire falls in flakes like snow		
The fire kills people and burns things up		
Further deaths are caused by smoke		
The smoke comes from 'heaven'		
It seems to cause an infectious (catching) disease		
The disease is spread by 'a foul blast of wind'		

2 Look at the map on page 5. Do travellers **A** and **B** agree about where these things happened? Suggest where it was.
3 Which shore does traveller **A** refer to? (You may have two or three ideas to discuss with your friends.)
4 Sometimes one person gets a story from someone else and alters it. Pretend this happened with travellers **A** and **B** and try to decide which of them had the story first.

The Plague hits Genoa

Let us imagine we are in the Italian port of Genoa early in 1348. The townsfolk have heard the travellers' tales of strange events and dreadful diseases. They are frightening tales, but they come from far-away countries such as China.

They are also worried by something else. No cargo boats have called at the port for several weeks. This is strange, for normally there are ships arriving all the time, laden with sun-dried grapes, spices and cloth. The busy harbour has fallen asleep, and Genoa's merchants have nothing to sell.

One morning, the people are startled awake by merchants dashing through the narrow streets on their horses and carts. Sometimes the merchants try to stand up hoping to get a glimpse of the Mediterranean Sea through the gaps between buildings. Yes, there are the sails! Three great ships are on the horizon. They are coming over the edge of the world to call at Genoa!

The wind blows strong and cold on the merchants' faces. They know it will soon blow the ships into harbour. They whip their horses, for all of them want to get there first. People leap into passage-ways as the carts hurtle by. A dying rat is crushed by a wheel. Pieces of dung and rotten fruit get stuck to the wheels and are thrown in the air. The merchants can think of nothing except the three tall ships. When they reach the quayside they do not talk as they usually do. They stay on their carts, silent and tense, as if they are waiting to start a race. There will be a race when they see where the first ship is going to dock, for whichever merchant gets there first can buy all the goods.

As the ships approach, the merchants see the sailors climbing the rigging to furl the sails. Soon they are far above the decks, jerking about on the rope-ladders. They look like flies in spiders' webs. They untie ropes and fold most of the sails away, in order to slow the ships down and therefore prevent them from smashing into the harbour wall.

But something is wrong. The merchants stare at one of the ships in disbelief. Can it be true? Is there only one man to do all the work? The ship needs ten or twenty men to sail it properly. The merchants watch as the lonely figure climbs a rope-ladder. Suddenly, the ladder jerks in a gust of wind. Dizzy with the height, the sailor begins to lose his grip.

7

He keeps a hand and foot in place but his body swings outwards. The merchants watch as he turns like a weather-vane. Then they see a mighty wave hit the ship on one side, causing it to tilt. The sailor is left hanging over the sea, he screams and falls, and the merchants see him disappear beneath the foam. Now his ship is out of control. It races towards the other ships, threatening to ram them. Then it swerves in a gust of wind, leaning over so far that its ropes and masts become entangled with some fishing boats. It rights itself, lifting two of them out of the water, smashes two others and then ploughs into a muddy beach.

As the ship comes to rest the merchants begin to whip their horses. If there really is no one on board they can fight for the goods and have them for nothing! They reach the ship and scramble aboard going below the decks to grab the goods. Almost at once they start to scramble up again, screaming and crying. There is something coming up behind them. It is chasing them across the deck. The merchants leap clear and we see that the thing is a man with peculiar marks and swellings all over his body. The first case of plague has reached Genoa.

Signs of the Death

Here are two reports about how the Plague affected people. They come from notes that were written by people who saw the disease – but escaped it themselves. One man wrote:

> *The mortality . . . lasted seven months. It was of two types. The first lasted two months, with continuous fever and spitting of blood, and from this one died in three days. The second lasted for the rest of the period, also with continuous fever but with swellings and boils, principally in the armpits and groin. From this one died in five days.*
> *La Grand Chirurgie*, ed. Nicaise, 1890

The other man wrote that after the buboes (swellings and boils) had appeared on the body:

> *Black or reddish spots often appeared on the arm, the thigh or in other places. Sometimes they were few and large, sometimes they were tiny but numerous. And just as the swellings had been an unfailing sign of approaching death, so were the spots . . .*
> Boccaccio: *Decameron*, tr. J.M. Rigg, 1930

Questions

1   There were two sorts of plague, pneumonic plague (which attacked the lungs) and bubonic plague (which affected other parts of the body). How could you tell which sort of plague a person had?

*Dutch woodcarving of a
plague victim*

2 Which symptom caused the Plague to be known as the Black
Death?
3 ·Now look at the picture above. What sort of plague does the
person depicted have?
4 In the story, a dying sailor accidentally terrifies the merchants.
What sort of plague does the sailor have?

Dirt and disease

Soon the Plague was sweeping through Europe. Sometimes the rats seemed to catch it first. In the following passage a modern author describes how they died:

> *They began to come out in the light of day and die in front of the horrified people. At night, too, in passages and alleys, their shrill little death-cries were clearly heard. In the morning the bodies were found in the gutters, each with a spot of blood, like a red flower, on its pointed nose. Some were swollen and beginning to rot, others were stiff with their whiskers erect.*
>
> Camus: *La Peste* (tr. as *The Plague* by S. Gilbert, 1965)

People were used to seeing dead rats, but this was different. They knew that the Plague would start killing humans and then they would be dying like the rats.

Few people except the authorities realised that filth and dirt helped diseases to spread. Some of the leading citizens knew, but communicating this was very hard. They could impose fines for putting 'dunghills, carrion or other stinking filth in the highway' – but where else could poor people empty the buckets they used at night?

Bad food helped to make things worse. Meat was poor because cattle and sheep were dropping dead in the fields from *murrain* (their own form of plague): 'Their bodies were so corrupted by the Plague that neither bird nor beast would touch the flesh.' Butchers sold it just the same! They hung the meat outside their shops, and often it was covered in flies when the customer bought it. Once again the law-makers tried to put things right. One law forbade the selling of meat that was 'putrid, rotten, stinking and abominable to the human race'. Sometimes butchers slaughtered animals outside their shops. In London, a royal proclamation complained of 'putrid blood running down the streets, and the bowels cast into the Thames'. As a result, said the proclamation:

> *Abominable and most filthy stinks . . . sickness and many other evils have happened to such as have abode in the city . . . and great dangers are feared to fall out for the time to come.*
>
> B. Lambert: *History and Survey of London*, 1806

People knew that something dreadful was going to happen, but what could they do?

In some cities the rich paid beggars to clean the streets. Each day they could earn a coin or two by collecting dead rats and dumping them outside the city. Some made brooms and used them to clear other rotting debris from the gutters. The job was really a waste of time, for above their heads a window might open at any moment, and a new lot of slops would splatter into the street below.

Rattus rattus; the black rat which carried the Plague

Sentries stood at the city gates only letting people in if they seemed to be healthy. When merchants came from neighbouring cities everyone crowded round them for news. How near was the Plague? Was it four towns away, or only three? Although sentries kept out anyone who seemed to be ill, rats could still squeeze through the smallest chink in the city walls. The scuffling sound of rats at night was nothing new, but now when people heard a rat in the straw of their beds they began to feel frightened. They thought of the dying rats in the street and how they could bring the Death right into their houses too.

Rats and fleas

In the fourteenth century the authorities knew two important things about the Plague: it seemed to thrive in dirty conditions and it often passed from victim to victim. This explains why they sometimes tried to clean their streets. It also explains why they tried to keep sick travellers out.

No one knew that fleas were a vital link between victims. If a rat died of plague its fleas would leave, and some would start to live on humans. When they sucked the humans' blood they injected into it the plague germs that had come from the rat.

11

But how did the Plague spread all the way across Europe and Asia? Most historians point to the fact that ships were often infested with rats. If the rats died of plague their fleas would give it to people in all the ports of call. In this way a ship could take plague from country to country – until the sailors died of it themselves. In addition to this, diseased rats could get into merchants' caravans (wagon trains). These could carry plague across country – away from the ports.

The idea above is known as the trade route theory. According to this, the coasts would be infected first, and plague would spread inland. It would close in on places like central England and central Spain. Landlocked countries would probably get it last of all.

Using the evidence: the Plague spreads to Britain
Let us look at the work of one historian who seems to believe the trade route theory, for he says the Plague was 'falling first . . . everywhere, on the seaports and estuaries'. Now let us look at his detailed account of how it spread through France and Britain. The map will help us to follow what he says:

estuaries: river mouths

A *In the spring [of 1348] it reached Gascony. . .*
B *Soon afterwards it broke out in Paris. . .*
C *By July, creeping . . . through Poitou and Brittany and round the coasts, it was in Normandy. . .*
D *Some time that August it broke out in the little Dorset coast town of Melcombe Regis, now Weymouth. . .*
E *Within a few weeks it reached Bristol, probably by sea, turning it into a cemetery. . .*
F *During that autumn the plague struck down southern shire after southern shire [but] the counties of Hampshire and Surrey . . . escaped the infection almost till Christmas. . .*
G *The plague reached London at the beginning of November. . .*
H *By the spring of 1349 it had reached Norfolk. In Acle church a . . . Latin inscription relates how that summer 'the brute beast plague' raged 'hour by hour'. . . The midlands suffered almost as badly.*
J *Before the summer ended the plague had crossed the Humber. In the West Riding nearly half the priests died; in the East Riding almost as many. . .*
K *Scotland, protected by a hundred miles of moorland, escaped until the end of the year. . .*
L *Next year it was the turn of the Welsh mountain valleys, and 'at last, as if sailing thither, the plague reached Ireland . . .'*

A. Bryant: *The Age of Chivalry,* 1963

Map of Great Britain and
western France

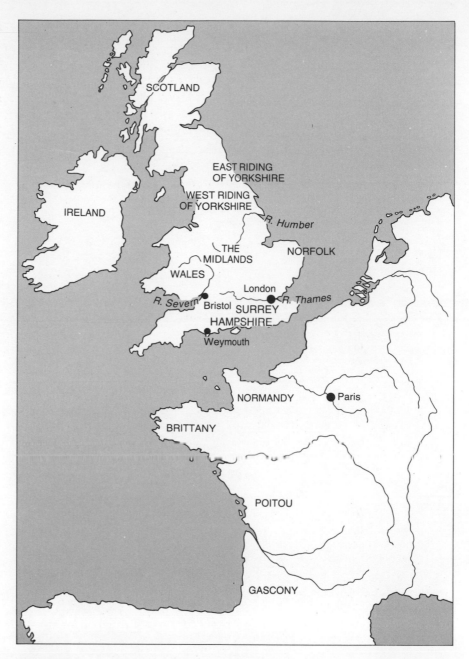

Questions

1 Draw a map similar to that shown here and mark in the dates at
   which the Plague first visited each area.
2 In which direction – roughly – did the Plague spread through
   England and Scotland? How long did it take?
3 Does this pattern agree with the trade route theory?
4 Ships from France were always arriving at ports all around the
   British coast, so would we expect the Plague to spread in the
   way it did? If not what would we expect instead?

Maps giving differing views of how the Plague spread

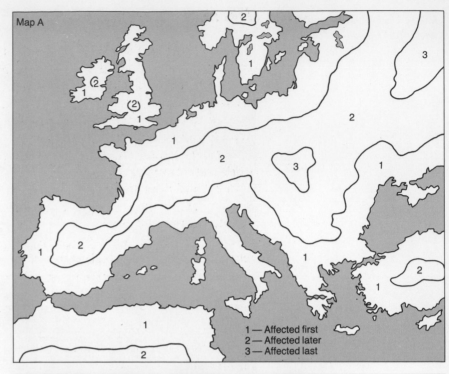

Map A

1 — Affected first
2 — Affected later
3 — Affected last

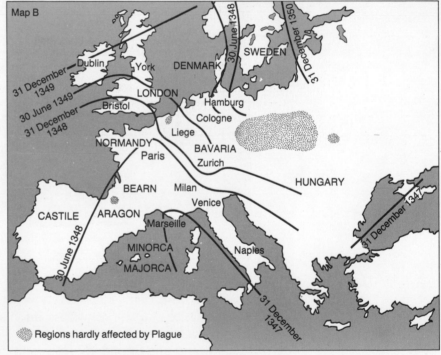

Map B

31 December 1349
30 June 1349
31 December 1348
30 June 1348
31 December 1347
31 December 1347
30 June 1348
31 December 1350

Dublin
York
DENMARK
SWEDEN
LONDON
Hamburg
Bristol
Cologne
Liege
NORMANDY
BAVARIA
Paris
Zurich
HUNGARY
BEARN
Milan
CASTILE
ARAGON
Venice
Marseille
MINORCA
Naples
MAJORCA

Regions hardly affected by Plague

Death from space?

Two scientists looked at the dates when the Plague arrived in different parts of Europe. They decided that the trade route theory was false. It seemed to them that the Plague had rolled across land and sea in a steady way. It had not appeared in the sea-ways first, for some ports seemed to be affected from inland. The scientists felt that trade had done little to spread the disease.

Their own idea was totally different. They suggested that as the world swept through space a cloud of dust and plague-germs must have entered the atmosphere somewhere far above the earth's surface. As the germs floated downwards they began to spread out. Because of this, the plague-infected area grew as time went on. Rats caught the disease, and their fleas passed it on to human beings. Even so, merchants with rats in their ships and caravans had little to do with its general spread across half the world. Each region had obtained its own batch of germs direct from the sky.

Questions

Study the two maps opposite:

1 Which map matches the trade route theory?
   Which map matches the scientists' theory?
2 The theories cannot both be correct. You know several facts about how the Plague spread through France and Great Britain. Which map and theory do these facts support?

15

2

THE PLAGUE IN CITIES

Disposing of the bodies

How did people behave when the Plague struck their city? At first, perhaps, they whispered and watched as the tell-tale signs began to appear. One family failed to open its shop, another sent for herbs and ancient remedies, but refused to say what the trouble was.

All at once, the citizens panicked. Some galloped off to their country homes, others tried to limit the Plague to the houses which were already infected. In one Italian city, Milan, a frenzied crowd set beggars to work nailing planks across the victims' doors and windows. The families cried for mercy and waved their hands till the last chink was closed. Now they were prisoners; and as they died of the Plague or starvation their homes became tombs for their festering bodies. In a neighbouring city healthy people spent their money on stocks of food then fetched wood and bricks and started shutting themselves up in a similar way. We can understand their reason for this if we listen to people who lived at the time:

> *The catching nature of the disease is indeed the most dreadful of all the terrors, for when anyone . . . is infected by it . . . all who see him in his sickness, or visit him, or do any business with him, or even carry him to the grave, quickly follow him there.*
> *The sick are served by their kinsfolk as dogs would be. Food is put near the bed . . . then they all run away.*
> De Smet: Recueil des Chroniques de Flandres, vol. 3

> *Everything which came from their bodies let off an unbearable stench: sweat, diarrhoea, spittle, breath – all so foul as to be overpowering.*
> J.P. Papon: De la Peste ou Epoques mémorables de ce Fleau

Perhaps it is not surprising that some people let their own relatives die unattended. Whatever they did, they were likely to catch the Plague themselves, for no precautions had any effect. In Milan the citizens gave up shutting the sick away, for the Plague seemed able to pass through walls.

Soon it was hard to avoid the Plague, for the sick were everywhere. In the streets people had to skirt round the bodies of those who had fallen, dying or dead. There were bodies in many doorways too, sometimes three or four lay together – a family group. The writer Boccaccio tells us about the countless dead in the city of Florence:

contamination: catching the disease

> *Most of the neighbours, moved . . . by fear of contamination . . . dragged the corpses out of the houses with their own hands . . . and*

Victims of the Black Death buried in their hundreds at Tournai

biers: coffins
in default: failing that

laid them round in front of the doors, where anyone that made the round might have seen, especially in the morning, more of them than he could count.

Afterwards they would have biers brought up or, in default, planks whereon they laid them. And on many occasions the same bier carried two or three corpses at once . . . one bier sufficing for husband and wife, two or three brothers, father and son, and so forth.

And times without number it happened that, as two priests bearing the cross were on their way to perform a funeral for someone, three or four biers were brought up at the rear by beggars; so that whereas the priests supposed that they had but one corpse to bury, they discovered that there were six, or eight, or sometimes more . . . It was come to this, that a dead man was of no more account than a dead goat would be today.

Boccaccio: *Decameron*, tr. J.M. Rigg, 1930

In another Italian city, Siena, things were completely out of hand:

No-one could be found to bury the dead for money or for friendship . . . And in many places great pits were dug and piled deep with huge heaps of the dead . . . And I, Agnolo di Tura, called the Fat, buried my five children with my own hands, and so did many others likewise. And there were also many dead throughout the city who were so sparsely covered with earth that the dogs dragged them forth and devoured their bodies.

Cronica Senese di A. di Tura del Grasso, Muratori 15

Life was turning into a nightmare. Some people's minds were crazed by fear; the disease itself sent others mad. In southern France a man climbed onto the roof of his house and threw down the tiles while someone on another roof did a crazy dance. Hysterical people started to imagine all sorts of things:

> *A column of fire was seen above the palace at Avignon, and a ball of fire was seen in the skies above Paris. In Venice a violent earth tremor set the bells of St Marks ringing without touch of human hand.*
>
> Philip Zeigler: *The Black Death*, 1969

people began seeing things

Questions

1 Why did healthy people sometimes shut themselves away?
2 How did people treat their sick relatives? Why?
3 Suggest one or two reasons why Agnolo di Tura could not find anyone to bury his children.
4 Dead people were being treated as of no importance. Find three or four examples of this in the things Boccaccio and Agnolo say.
5 Why should people be very upset by the tolling of bells? (Priests were ringing them all the time, but in the end some councils forbade it.)
6 Look at the pictures. What are the artists trying to say?

Was the Plague sent by God?

Many believed that God was using the Plague as a way of ending the world. Others believed he was using it to punish wrong-doing. Here are the words of an English priest called Henry of Knighton:

> *In those days [at the start of the Plague] many people were very upset because, when jousting competitions were held ... a band of women would arrive as if they had come to join the sport, dressed in a variety of the most lavish male costumes. They even wore ... knives in pouches slung across their bodies; and thus they rode on choice war horses or other splendid steeds to the place of tournament. There and thus they spent or, rather, squandered their possessions, and wearied their bodies with fooleries and wanton buffoonery... But God, in this matter, as in all others, brought marvellous remedy.*
>
> Chronicon Henrici Knighton, c.1360

Fighting the Plague

Some people tried to end the Plague with prayers and religious services. Others tried to satisfy God by whipping themselves. These people, known as Flagellants, thought that God might spare the rest of mankind in return for their suffering. However most people only thought of themselves. Boccaccio tells us of some of the different things they did:

> *They banded together and ... formed communities in houses where there were no sick, and lived a separate and secluded life ... eating and drinking very moderately of the most delicate meats and the finest wines....*
>
> *Others ... maintained that to drink freely, to frequent places of public resort, and to take their pleasure with song and revel ... was the perfect remedy for so great an evil....*
>
> *They used the houses of others like inns, if they saw in them anything that was particularly to their taste or liking. They were readily able to do this because the owners, seeing death so close, had become as reckless of their property as of their lives; so that most of the houses were open to all-comers, and no distinction was observed between the stranger who presented himself and the rightful lord....*
>
> *The rule of law ... had almost ceased due to lack of [officials], most of whom, like the rest of the citizens, were either dead, sick, or so short of workers that they could not carry out any duties. Because of this each person was able to do as he thought fit.*
>
> Boccaccio: *Decameron*, tr. J.M. Rigg, 1930

Priests and doctors were as helpless as the city officials. A man called Simon of Covino said that

Often [...] while administering aid; and often [...] of the Plague-stricken person they [...] ey had come to assist.

[...] des Chartes, 1840–41, vol. 2

In the e[...] he sick! They argued among themselv[...] Plague at bay. Some recommended [...] or sweetly scented air, and many citizens walked around with their noses buried in bunches of flowers. Others recommended the breathing of offensive smells. People who followed this advice kept their noses [...] pile of dung. The doctors also argued [...] Some believed in cutting the buboes [...] pus run out. Others believed in applyin[...]ances.

Some [...] he city, but others fled to the countrys[...] country palace and spent his time bet[...] ther method of avoiding the Plague!

Usually it was the rich who left, for they were the ones with country homes. Many avoided a city death only to die in the countryside. Even so, the poor felt betrayed by those they had trusted. Death was rampant 'in market places and narrow streets', but it seemed to spare 'the broader and more spacious parts'.

[Handwritten note: Priests seized by plague as helping]

[Handwritten note: The pope ran and hid]

Questions

1 Look at the passage by Knighton on page 19. He disapproves of the women for several reasons. Try to decide what the reasons are. What does his final sentence mean?

2 Look at the pictures. Which shows a group of Flagellants? How can you tell?

3 In the other picture, how does the artist show that the Plague is raging dreadfully?

4 What marvellous sight has the bishop seen? What could it mean?

5 *Sceptre and crown*
   Shall tumble down
   And in the dust be equal made
   With the poor crooked scythe and spade.

   This rhyme sums up a number of things about the Plague. Try to say what they are.

len vnder auf peutlen vnd absoluierten selber
in ein ander vnd hielten vnd gepulen vil ay
ein ander zo haben bundeliche ding on falsh,
weiß vnd artiul vnder cristen gelauben vnd

3

THE PLAGUE IN THE ENGLISH COUNTRYSIDE

Bishop and reeve

We have seen how the Plague affected cities, but most of the population lived in the countryside. Let us look closely at what went on in some south of England villages close to Farnham.

The Bishop of Winchester owned all the land and cottages in this area, so the villagers had to pay him rent. They also gave him some of their crops and sometimes had to help with the work on his private estate, which included some of the finest land in the neighbourhood.

One of the Bishop's tenants had a special job – he acted as the Bishop's reeve, collecting payments and looking after the Bishop's estate. Although expenses swallowed up most of the money he gathered in, he had to finish up with a profit.

The Bishop was a kindly man, but he demanded a bigger profit every year to pay for having part of Winchester's old cathedral demolished, in order to replace it with something really grand. The money for this would have to come from the Bishop's estates and, of course, from the villagers, who paid their rents and dues.

When a tenant died, the reeve collected his finest beast and added it to the Bishop's herd. This form of death tax was known as *heriot*. In a normal year the reeve collected six or seven animals, but obviously the number varied according to how many tenants died.

In 1348 the Bishop decided that his reeve was getting too old for the job and replaced him with a man called Renwick. The old reeve died soon afterwards and Renwick collected his shaggy mare for the Bishop's estate. Renwick felt he had started well as mares were worth about nine shillings each – as much as good milch cows. Perhaps he would get another six heriots during the year. If he obtained a really fine animal every time, the Bishop might reward him with a giant cheese or a sack of barley. But things failed to go as Renwick expected. In his first year as reeve (from October 1348 to September 1349) he did not collect seven heriots – he collected 189! There were 26 horses, 54 cows and even a bull, as well as cheaper animals like sheep. As the number of animals grew and grew the Bishop did not seem pleased at all. His meadows were becoming over-crowded, the grass was disappearing fast, and sickly beasts would soon be dying all over the place like human beings. Renwick decided to drive all the extra livestock to market. The best thing to do was to get a good price for them.

At the market Renwick was in for a nasty shock; everyone else was selling, too. There were very few buyers, and he had to bring most of

milch: milk

Above: *Workers with sickles*

Below: *Aerial view of the outline of a 17th century village which was devastated by plague and which eventually disappeared.*

his animals home. He had sold 60 of his beasts, but at prices so low he wondered what the Bishop would say. He would certainly have to keep the rest.

Difficult times for the reeve

We can read in Renwick's account-sheet of how he finally found new pastures for 'the multitude of the Bishop's cattle which came from heriots'. This account also shows the cost of having a stable enlarged. Renwick bought:–

600 nails	5½d
2 hinges	1d
1 lock & bolt	3d

Wood was free as there were plenty of trees on the Bishop's estate. Two men were hired to do the work, and in five days the walls and the door were complete. Then, with a boy to hold their rickety ladder, they took another two days to add the roof. Their work was good, but they asked for a total of three shillings in wages. It was quite a lot more than the reeve had expected. He argued at first, but then decided he had better pay up as workers were getting very scarce and he could not risk upsetting them. If they lived, he might need their help another time.

Soon afterwards, Renwick had to pay a whole groat (a fourpenny piece) before anyone would go down a well to fetch a lost bucket. Then, in spite of the heavy cost, he had to hire two extra workers – a cowman and a shepherd boy – to tend the Bishop's growing herds. He took them on at lambing time, early in 1349. Twenty weeks later the workers were still alive. As for the Bishop, reports of his banquets showed that he was in splendid health. Renwick, however, looked very ill, and some people thought he was dying of the Plague, as his daughter had done. The truth was that Renwick was sick with worry. The Bishop's estate was losing money, rents were down, the income from sales was almost nil, and the wage bill was going up and up.

In one way the Bishop's greed was a help. At the end of the summer he asked for 100 oxen and cows to replenish his larder. Renwick had them killed, salted and sent away to Winchester. Now, at last, he could manage without the herdsman and the shepherd. Even so, things were getting worse and worse. During the year, 189 tenants had died. In 137 cases Renwick had found new tenants to take the place of the old. That meant 52 holdings (small rented farms) were empty. In his accounts Renwick used the Latin words *defectus per pestilentiam* (abandoned on account of the Plague).

The loss of rent was a serious matter but, worse than that, the land itself was being lost. Tenants were needed to stop the land – and the animals on it – becoming wild. Thistles were springing up already, and animals were straying into the empty cottages, as well as onto other plots. Renwick imagined ruin engulfing the whole estate, and

England becoming a jungle of weeds. This sort of thing had happened in some parts of Europe already. Travellers, merchants and pilgrims told of:

> cattle wandering without herdsmen in the fields, towns and waste-lands; [of] barns and wine-cellars standing wide open, houses empty and few people to be found anywhere... And in many different areas both plough-lands and fields lying uncultivated.
>
> De Smet: *Receuil des Chroniques de Flandres*, vol. 11

The clay-pit at Farnham became a den of foxes and wolves, for no one seemed to be making bricks or pots any more. Farnham fern (which brickmakers used to add to their clay) grew thick and unwanted all over the hills. Renwick decided to concentrate on the pasture land and fence in some of the wandering livestock. However, after failing to find any workers to help him he gave up the job of reeve in despair.

How prices rose

Let us look closely at how the Plague affected prices. Death caused a drop in the number of people making things and as a result manufactured goods like harnesses, nails, pots and pans became very scarce. If you look at the diagram below you will see that under **Quantity of Goods Available** the words big reduction are underlined.

The Plague killed a lot of the customers, too, but those who survived sometimes needed extra supplies of various things. For example, Renwick the reeve needed far more nails than ever before, and was lucky to manage without a new bucket. In general, the demand for goods was almost unchanged, so the words no change have been underlined in the column headed **Quantity of Goods Required**.

The arrow shows us what happened as people competed for the scarce supplies they needed so badly; they began to pay more in order to get them.

Quantity of Goods Available	Quantity of Goods Required	
big rise	big rise	
small rise	small rise	PRICES GO UP
no change	no change	
small reduction	small reduction	
big reduction	big reduction	

Using the evidence

1 The diagrams below are to be copied out and completed. The first will show how the Plague affected animal prices, the second will show how wages changed. When they are finished they should look like the one on the previous page, with one item underlined in each column. Link these items with an arrow and give the arrow a suitable label.

No. of Animals for Sale	No. of Animals Needed for Food	
big rise	big rise	
small rise	small rise	
no change	no change	
small reduction	small reduction	
big reduction	big reduction	

No. of Workers	Work to be Done	
big rise	big rise	
small rise	small rise	
no change	no change	
small reduction	small reduction	
big reduction	big reduction	

2 Look at Graph A on page 29 and work out roughly how many tenants died in the Farnham area between 1348 and 1352.
3 The district had about 700 tenants at the start of the Plague. Most had families, and this brought the total population to nearly 4 000. Estimate how many people died altogether.

TROUBLE IN STORE

The Statute of Labourers

By 1351 the Black Death was slowly fading away. Nearly half the people of Europe had died, but those who were left began to live as they had done before. At Farnham, there was a new reeve to run the Bishop's affairs, and he wrote his accounts on the same roll of paper that Renwick had used. At first it looked as though little had happened. The estate was making a profit again. There was just enough money to pay for new fences, and the sheep and cattle grazed contentedly. However, there was trouble simmering under the surface. At the height of the Plague King Edward III had sent out the following proclamation:

ordained: decreed

> *A great part of the people, and especially of labourers and servants, have died of the pestilence. Some, perceiving the pressing need of their lords, and the great scarcity of servants, refuse to work unless they receive excessive wages. . . .*
>
> *We have ordained that every man or woman in the realm . . . if he shall be required to serve in any suitable service . . . shall be bound to serve him who required him, and shall receive only such wages as were customary before the [Plague].*
>
> D. Hughes: *Illustrations of Chaucer's England*, 1919

Two years later, Parliament passed a law called The Statute of Labourers. This backed up the royal proclamation by adding the threat of punishments. Even so, many workers still demanded higher wages than ever before. Here is what Henry of Knighton tells us:

> *These labourers were so arrogant and hostile that they paid no heed to the King's command; but if anyone wanted to have them he was obliged to give them whatever they asked, either losing his fruits and crops or satisfying their greed and arrogance.*
>
> *But the King levied heavy fines upon abbots, priors, knights . . . and others great and small throughout the countryside when it became known to him that they disobeyed his ordinance, and gave higher wages to their labourers. . . .*
>
> *Then the King caused many labourers to be arrested, and sent them to prison . . .*
>
> D. Hughes: *Illustrations of Chaucer's England*, 1919

Questions

1 Look at the King's command. It applied to 'every man or woman in the realm', but poor people felt it picked on them. Why?

Graph A

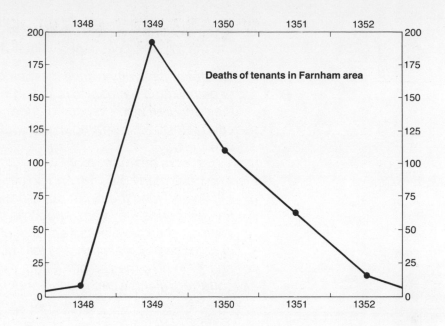

Deaths of tenants in Farnham area

Graph B

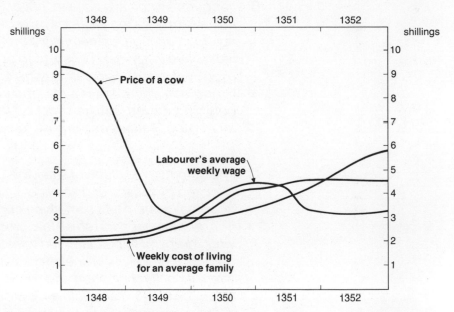

Price of a cow

Labourer's average weekly wage

Weekly cost of living for an average family

2   Look at Graph B. Did poor people need the higher wages they were getting in 1351? Why should this be?

3   How easily could poor people buy what they needed in 1352? How had things changed since the previous year? What had caused this change?

4   What critical words does Knighton use about labourers who 'paid no heed to the King's command'? Does he use any similar words about the abbots, priors and knights who also disobeyed the command?
    According to Knighton, what excuse do the rich people have for disobeying the command?

Using the evidence: victims or villains?
Look at the following passages written by contemporaries:

A *Whatever the women save by spinning they spend on rent, or on milk and oatmeal to make gruel and fill the bellies of their children who clamour for food. And they themselves are often famished with hunger and wretched with the miseries of winter. . . .*

    Yet there are many more who suffer like them – men . . . who have many children and no means but their trade to clothe and feed them. For many hands are waiting to grasp the few pence they earn, and while the friars feast on roast venison, they have bread and thin ale, and perhaps a scrap of cold meat or stale fish. . . I tell you, it would be a real charity to help men so burdened, and comfort these cottagers along with the blind and the lame. . .

                  Langland: *Piers the Ploughman*

B *Labourers who have no land, but only their shovels, would not dream of eating yesterday's vegetables. Cheap ale was not good enough for them, nor a hunk of bacon, but they must have fresh meat or fish, fried or baked and hot from the oven, lest they should catch a chill on their stomachs!*

    And so it is nowadays – the labourer is angry unless he gets high wages, and he . . . curses the king and his council for making Statutes on purpose to plague the workmen!

                  Langland: *Piers the Ploughman*

Statutes: laws

C *The common multitude of small folk . . . will never be checked by reason or discipline . . . the present world is so troubled by them that something ought to be done about it . . . For the poor and small folk, who should stick to their work, demand to be better fed than their masters. . . They bedeck themselves in fine colours and fine attire, whereas (were it not for their pride and secret conspiracies) they would be clad in sackcloth as of old. . . .*

    The shepherd and the cowherd demand more wages now than the reeve used to get; and labourers are now of such a price that, when we must needs use them, where we used to spend two shillings we must now spend five or six. . . .

    They work little, dress and feed like their betters, and ruin stares us in the face. It seems to me that the lords of this land are sunk in sleep and lethargy, so that they take no heed of the madness of the common folk. Thus they allow this nettle, that is so violent in itself, to grow . . . Soon – if God provides no remedy – [it] will suddenly sting us before men do justice upon it . . .

                  Gower (fourteenth century)

Questions

1   How does Langland make you pity the poor?
    How does he try to make you admire them?

2   Which people does Langland seem to dislike?
    How does he try to make fun of these people?

3   Do you think Gower was a peasant himself or a wealthy
    landowner? Give reasons for your answer.

4   In what ways is Gower unfair about the peasants' wages and
    how well off the peasants are?

5   What words does Gower use in his opening paragraph to
    suggest that the peasants are getting together and plotting?

6   In his final paragraph, what does Gower mean by 'this nettle'?
    Why should he choose these particular words?

7   Consider all the evidence presented in this chapter. Do you
    think the landless labourer was demanding too much pay?

Below left: *A painting of Edward III*

Below right: *A painting of Richard II*

31

Richard II succeeds to the throne

In every district the landowner held a court which dealt with local problems such as debts. In the years which followed the Black Death the courts issued more and more warrants for people's arrest. In many cases the person's offence was that he had 'removed himself outside the estate' – run away from the landlord. This was a very serious matter. The tenants were serfs, who ranked little better than slaves. As we have seen, they had to serve the lord of the manor, and pay him many fees and dues, and in addition to this they could not leave the district without his permission. He regarded them as property, like trees and cows.

In 1377 Richard II became King of England, and although he was only ten years old his wealthier subjects wanted him to deal with the serfs. They told him what had been going on:

> *These peasants have refused to let their landlords' officials collect the usual dues and services; they have plotted and agreed together to resist the lords and their officials by force, so that each will aid the other whenever they are called upon for any reason . . . As a result, for fear of the deaths which could follow from the rebellion and resistance of these men, the lords and their officials do not compel them to give their dues and services.*
>
> Dobson: *Peasants' Revolt*

Unpopular taxes

Richard and his Parliament ignored the unrest between landlords and tenants. They were more concerned with charging taxes to pay for the war against the French which was raging at that time. In 1377 they made each adult pay a groat (fourpence). In 1379 poor people paid another groat, while rich people paid up to 50 groats. It worked out at roughly three groats per person. The rich paid more and the poor paid less, but three groats was the average payment over the country.

In 1381 Parliament asked the tax collectors to bring in the same amount again. The rich had to pay up to 60 groats while the poor had to pay at least one. The important thing was for the people of every town and village to pay an average of three groats apiece.

Tax collectors visited every town in the country, and sent their assistants around all the villages. They began their work by listing the adults in each locality. When the collector knew how many adults there were in a certain place he multiplied the number by three. This told him how many groats were required. The biggest amounts came from wealthy folk such as landlords and merchants. The poor folk had to pay the rest.

Now look at the chart; it shows you how the tax was shared out in the two Suffolk villages of Brockley and Chevington. In each case the taxman had 70 people on his list, so he had to collect 3 × 70 groats from each village. The totals (210) were the same, but these concealed very serious differences.

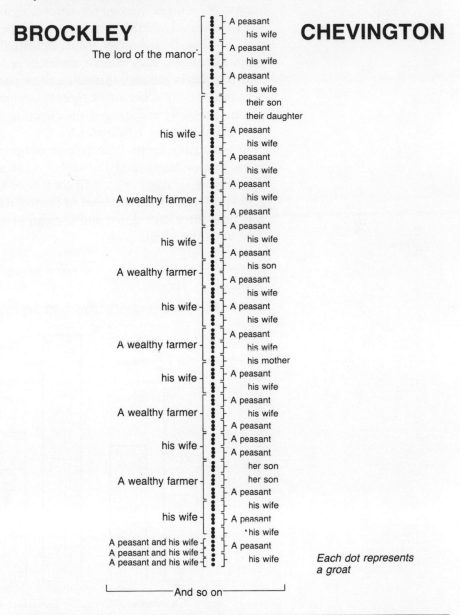

BROCKLEY

The lord of the manor

his wife

A wealthy farmer

his wife

A wealthy farmer

his wife

A wealthy farmer

his wife

A wealthy farmer

his wife

A wealthy farmer

his wife

A peasant and his wife
A peasant and his wife
A peasant and his wife

And so on

CHEVINGTON

A peasant
his wife
A peasant
his wife
A peasant
his wife
their son
their daughter
A peasant
his wife
A peasant
his wife
A peasant
his wife
A peasant
A peasant
his wife
A peasant
his son
A peasant
his wife
A peasant
his wife
A peasant
his wife
his mother
A peasant
his wife
A peasant
his wife
A peasant
A peasant
A peasant
her son
her son
A peasant
his wife
A peasant
his wife
A peasant
his wife
A peasant
his wife

Each dot represents a groat

Questions

1 How much did each poor person in Brockley have to pay? How much did each poor person in Chevington have to pay?
2 Why did they have to pay different amounts?
3 How did the rules for the tax of 1381 differ from those for the tax of 1379?

Cheating the taxman

The tax collectors had made lists of taxpayers in 1377. When they compared these earlier lists with the later ones they could see that some people had avoided paying any tax at all. The bar-chart below shows the tell-tale figures for three English counties.

Men cheated in 1381 by failing to tell the tax officials of other adults who lived in their houses. Most admitted having wives, but few of them mentioned their elderly mothers or grown-up children (unmarried daughters normally lived in their parents' homes).

Often, the tax collector's helper was a local man – a reeve, perhaps – and he probably encouraged the cheating. It seems to have happened in every county in England.

The cheating shows how defiant and poor many people were. They were sick of taxes, and the tax of 1381 was very unfair. To make matters worse, wages were still controlled by law, but prices were not. Laws and landlords even tried to control the lives of the poorer folk. It was time for a showdown and it came in 1381, when taxmen tried to deal with the cheats.

Questions

1   Look at the bar-chart. How had the totals changed since 1377?

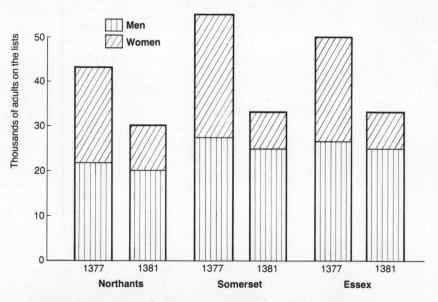

2   What was suspicious about the way the figures for 1381 were made up?
3   Study the information about Chevington on page 33. Do you think some of the villagers cheated? What makes you think so?
4   Why were these villagers so eager to dodge the tax of 1381?

LONDON BEWARE!

The King and the Commons

The year was 1381 and the month of May was coming to a sunny end. Thomas Bampton stood nervously in the little tithe-hall at Brentwood in Essex. In front of him was a rough wooden table upon which were spread various tax-lists. This was all that lay between him and an angry crowd of 100 men who had gathered from the neighbouring villages. He cleared his throat and announced that he had come on behalf of Robert Hales, the man who collected the nation's tax. He wanted to find out whether certain local villages had underpaid the latest demand. He said he would start with Fobbing, a village, according to the list, that seemed to have no women. Someone shouted a rude remark and someone else waved a piece of paper – a receipt for the tax already paid – and cried, 'And not a penny more will you get.' Bampton replied that prison awaited those who had not paid a penny to start with. We do not know exactly what followed this unwise remark. Maybe the people surged forward in anger, pushing the table, pinning Bampton against the wall and turning him into a prisoner himself. At all events the meeting ended in uproar before it had really begun.

Bampton finally got back to London, covered in bruises, to report on what had occurred. A judge called Robert Belknap set out straight away to deal with the villagers. However, two London butchers also set out. They galloped ahead and rode around Fobbing and neighbouring villages, warning them that Belknap was on his way with at least three companions, and urged people to grab knives and axes.

When Belknap arrived he tried to set up a new enquiry. Straight away the villagers seized the judge, his assistants and the local men who were going to act as witnesses. In front of the judge they beat all the other men to death. They hacked off the victims' heads with their axes, jammed them on poles and paraded them around the locality. As for the judge, they made him swear that he would never hold such an enquiry again. Then they released him, hoping, perhaps, that this would help to calm things down.

They knew that they must still expect official revenge. It could well be ferocious. Perhaps a company of soldiers would come out and try to kill them all. They prepared for this by increasing their strength, both in numbers and weapons. They also set about plundering the estates of the wealthy. In this way they could right old wrongs and settle local grievances, although they might not live to enjoy the benefits.

To the great surprise of the Essex rebels nothing happened. Then their informers told them why. The peasants of Kent were rebelling too, and in London itself the King and his ministers 'felt the ground quaking beneath their feet'.

The Kentish leader was Abel Ker, who had led a band of rioters into Dartford and 'traitorously moved the men of the said town to take part in a rising, making divers assemblies and gatherings against the King's peace.' Robert Cave, a Dartford baker, led the rioters on into Rochester, where they overwhelmed the castle, broke into the dungeons and freed – 'against his will' – a man who had been imprisoned for running away from his master's estate.

moved: spurred on
making divers assemblies: having various meetings

On 7 June the Kentish rebels poured into Maidstone, and there 'they chose as chief Wat Tyler of that place'. By now they were probably 10 000 strong, and attracting additional men all the time. They smashed their way into Maidstone jail, which belonged to Simon Sudbury, the Archbishop of Canterbury, and freed his prisoners, some of whom joined the rebel mob. Then they made wealthy and important people swear an oath of loyalty to 'the King and the Commons' (the common folk).

Rebellion was spreading throughout the land. In many counties townsfolk and countryfolk banded together, just as they were doing in Kent. All were sick of Hales and his taxes. To make matters worse, certain towns like St Albans and Bury St Edmunds belonged to their local monasteries. The citizens there were serfs just like the country-folk. They were jealous because a lot of towns had gained their freedom from such monasteries, but, where a town had also gained a selfish mayor and councillors its people might be just as unhappy.

'The mad priest of Kent'

One of the prisoners freed from the jail at Maidstone was a wandering priest by the name of John Ball. His enemies called him 'the mad priest of Kent'. The Archbishop of Canterbury was his bitterest foe. This is how he explained his reasons for locking Ball up:

> *He had slunk [here], like the fox that evades the hunter, and feared not to preach and argue both in churches and churchyards (without the leave or against the will of the church authorities) and also in markets and other such places, there deceiving the ears of the people by his rantings, and putting about scandals concerning me and other bishops and clergy. What is more, he has used concerning the Pope himself dreadful language such as shocked the ears of good Christians.*
>
> Quoted by Oman in: *The Great Revolt of 1381*, 1906

Ball was now free, and was able to spur the rebels on with his clever ideas and arguments. He started one of his speeches in rhyme:

> *When Adam delved and Eve spun*
> *Who was then the gentleman?*

He went on to say that the rebels should follow Adam's example, digging the land and destroying weeds. The rest of the speech made the meaning clear. However, Ball wrote letters, too, and these were often puzzling from beginning to end. He used secret agents to smuggle these letters to rebels in other parts of the country, for the trouble had spread as far north as Scarborough. One letter started:

> *John Ball greets you well all, and does you to understand that he has rung your bell.*

Another was even more peculiar:

> *John Schepe ... greets well John Nameless, and John the Miller, and John the Carter, and bids them ... that they stand together in God's name, and bids Piers Ploughman go to his work, and chastise [punish] well Hob the robber, and take with you John Trueman and all his fellows and no more. And look you shape to one head and no more.*

Closing in on London

The rebels began to close in on London. The Essex rebels approached from the north while Tyler, Ball and the Kentish rebels approached from the south. On 12 June both groups arrived. The Kentish contingent thronged the southern bank of the Thames. The city lay on the other side of the river, and the Mayor's officials had raised London Bridge's central drawbridge. Unable to cross, the rebels went on the

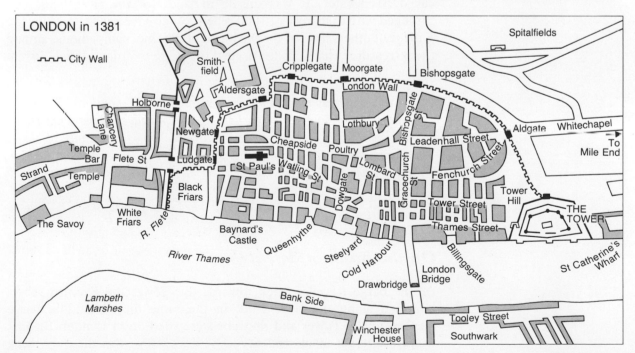

LONDON in 1381

37

Richard II speaking to the rebels, taken from Froissart's chronicle

rampage. They broke open prisons, ransacked the Archbishop's palace and, as Londoners watched from across the river, set houses blazing throughout the night.

The teenage King and his chief advisers had a very clear but frightening view. They had shut themselves up in the Tower of London. This meant they could also see the camp-fires of the Essex rebels just outside the city gates. There was no wide river to keep these other rebels back. The city was doomed!

Richard decided to do what he could. When morning broke he asked his bargemen to row him down-river as he wished to parley with some of the Kentish leaders. Ten minutes' rowing carried them clear of all the smoke, and they drew towards the southern shore at a place called Blackwater. It was unsafe to land, for the river bank was thronged with as many as 10 000 rebels. Some gave loyal cheers for the King, but others howled for the blood of his chief companions, among them treasurer Hales. Hales begged the King to order a quick retreat to the Tower:

> *The rebels thereupon burst out into curses and wild shouts of 'Traitor! Traitor!' but did not, as might have been expected, send the departing boat on its way with a volley of arrows. The first minute of the rowing, however, must have been one of deadly terror for the royal party. They might every one of them have been riddled with shafts before the barge had got out of range.*
>
> Oman: *The Great Revolt of 1381*, 1906

On the brink of defeat

As the barge travelled back towards the Tower the Kentish rebels swarmed along the river bank in the same direction. The barge berthed at the Tower and the rebels crowded on to London Bridge, desperate to get inside the city. The drawbridge was the only thing that held them back. They knew that they must enter now or return home defeated. Their urgency was heightened by lack of food. The journey by foot from Kent had taken two days, they had spent another day on the outskirts of London and in all this time had not had a meal to keep them going. No wonder they were desperate to cross the bridge. Perhaps they could lower the drawbridge themselves but how could they overpower the guards that had been posted? There were only a few, but enough to hold the narrow bridge. A report written shortly after the riots tells us that the rebels were in a mind to return to their homes. Then everything changed. The drawbridge was lowered and the rebels began to pour into London, begging, buying and stealing all the food and drink the city possessed. Soon they were ready for the violent and bloody work which lay ahead. Many had long-bows, while others now seized hammers and axes.

Using the evidence: entering London

How had the rebels got into London? At the time it seemed a mystery, and all sorts of ideas and rumours sprang up. Here are some that were written down soon after the riots:

A   *The commons of Southwark rose with [the rebels] and cried to the guards . . . to lower the drawbridge and let them in, or otherwise they should be undone. And for fear that they had of their lives, the guards let them enter, much against their will.*
    Anonimal Chronicle

B   *Witnesses say that . . . . Walter Sybyle, then an alderman, knowing and seeing the people to be doing such fierce and wicked evils in Southwark, on this Thursday [13th June] stood in arms on London Bridge. However, he sent back several men who were willing to help . . . declaring openly, 'These Kentish men are friends to us and to the King.' And so, like a treacherous criminal, he let the . . . mob in.*
    Report by Sheriffs and Jurors of London, Nov. 20, 1382

C   *All London, except for the rebels, was in terror. When they approached the city the mayor and the richer citizens held council and decided to close the gates and let no-one in; but they decided on reflection that there would then be a danger of all the suburbs being burned to the ground. So the city remained open to them, and they entered in troops of anything from 20 to 200 depending on the size of the towns from which they came.*
    Froissart

D   *Walworth the mayor had closed the gate of Aldgate . . . lest the evil-doers of Essex should enter . . . [but] on Wednesday [June 12th] William Tonge, then an alderman, opened the*

gate by night and let the mobs come in. And as soon as they were inside the city they mixed with the evil-doers from Kent....
Report by Sheriffs and Jurors of London, Nov. 20, 1382

E *For a fortnight before the entry of the Essex rioters into London a pair of butchers called Adam Atwell and Roger Harry had been whipping them up and spurring them on. Afterwards, on the day of the feast of Corpus Christi [June 13th] they brought these rioters into the city.*
Report by Sheriffs and Jurors of London, Nov. 20, 1382

1 Copy out the table and then indicate which reports agree with each statement by inserting their letters in the right hand column.

Statement	Report
Officials decided to let the rebels enter the city They tried to keep the rebels out	
There were loyal guards on London Bridge Sybyle prevented the bridge being guarded	
The rebels had done a lot of damage in Southwark The people of Southwark supported the rebels	
The Kentish rebels had already entered London by the night of June 12th The Kentish rebels entered the city on June 13th	
The Essex rebels entered during the night of June 12th, after being shut out They entered London on June 13th, during the day, without any difficulty	
The rebels and their supporters were evil	

2 Discuss the reports and the ways in which they agree or disagree with each other. Try to explain two or three of the disagreements.
3 Imagine you are writing a book on the Peasants' Revolt. Make a subheading: 'How the rebels entered London' and draft out a paragraph to explain. Then write a polished paragraph for your teacher to read.

6 GOING HOME EMPTY-HANDED

Revenge at last!

Soon the rebels were taking revenge on the men they hated most of all. They had freed the Archbishop's prisoners and burnt his palace but the Archbishop was safe, for the moment, in the Tower of London with Hales and the King. John of Gaunt, the Duke of Lancaster, was also safe – he was staying in Scotland. He owned more land (and ruled more peasants) than anyone else except the King. His palace, the Savoy, in London, was the most magnificent dwelling in England. The rebels knew that Gaunt was rich through the sweat and toil of his helpless tenants. By mid-afternoon they were breaking down the doors of the palace. Some went inside and started throwing furniture and other property out of the windows while the rebels outside dashed it to pieces on the cobbled street or smashed it with axes. They tore the curtains and hangings to shreds and shattered precious stones on the cobbles with hammers.

The rebels' ideal was to do away with all this wealth. They did not want to seize it themselves. One rebel did try to steal a silver bowl, but other rebels grabbed him and put him to death on the spot. Even so, a strong-box containing £1 000 was smuggled over a rear wall into a little boat on the River Thames. These thieves too were caught in the end. Another selfish group of rebels spent a merry time in the cellars, for the Duke had excellent stocks of wine. When, in the end, the others set the palace ablaze, they died there in a drunken heap. Some of the barrels had gunpowder in them instead of wine, and these exploded amid the flames.

The rioters now set off for the Temple, the place where London's lawyers lived, studied, and did their work. Oman records that the rioters wrecked and destroyed whole libraries of deeds and documents and that:

> It was marvellous to see how even the most aged and infirm of the lawyers scrambled off with the agility of rats or evil spirits.

Hales had close connections with the Temple of Law, but the rioters felt that they should punish him further. They went on the rampage at various mansions and institutions owned by Hales or under his rule. The rioters wanted Hales himself but he stayed in the Tower.

The meeting at Mile End Meadow

During the night the King sent a message to some of the rebel leaders. He asked them to meet him at Mile End Meadow, just outside the city walls. The leaders agreed, and at seven o'clock the following morning he rode from the Tower. He had some guards and advisers with him,

Rebels having a 'merry time' in the cellar of a great house

but Hales and the Archbishop of Canterbury stayed behind for safety's sake. The meeting went smoothly, though chroniclers say that 60 000 rebels were there as well as their leaders. Froissart records that:

Richard asked pleasantly, 'Friends, I am your King and your lord. What do you want? And what do you wish to say?'

Those who heard him answered, 'We want you to set us free forever, us and our descendants and our lands, and grant that we should never again be called serfs, nor held in bondage.'

They explained that most of the rebel farmers would gladly pay a modest rent of 4d an acre every year. They must, however, be totally free of the landlord's control. They would make no other payments whatsoever, nor would they owe the landlord either service or obedience. They would be able to move to another district whenever they wanted. Froissart's account states that:

Richard proclaimed to them that he would confirm and grant it that they should be free, and generally should have their will, and that they might go through all the realm of England and catch all traitors and bring them to him in safety, and then he would deal with them as the law demanded.

All the innocent and well-intentioned people were quite satisfied by these words, and began to return to London ... and the King gave orders for 30 secretaries to draw up the letters that very day, and for the letters to be sealed and handed over.

The chief mischief-makers, however, remained: Tyler, Straw and Ball declared that though the people were satisfied, they themselves would not depart. And with them there remained over 30 000 who took the same view; they stayed in the city, showing no inclination to receive the King's letters, but keeping London in a state of terror.

Questions
1   Look at the extracts above. What does the writer think of the King? How can you tell?
2   Who is the new leader mentioned in the second extract?
3   The writer calls some of the rebels 'innocent and well-intentioned'. What is he trying to say about the *other* rebels?
4   What are the 'letters' mentioned in the second extract?
5   According to the second extract, Tyler, Straw and Ball admit that the people are 'satisfied'. What makes this seem rather unlikely?
6   The rebels wanted to deal with those they regarded as 'traitors'. How was the King cautious in what he said about this?

Storming the Tower

When Tyler finally left the meadow he led a band of angry rebels straight to the Tower. The rebels did not try to hurt the guards. They shook their hands and stroked their beards in a cheeky way, telling them that in future days all men would be brothers. Unsure which side they ought to be on, the bewildered guards allowed them to enter.

The rebels did not show brotherly love to Hales or Sudbury. They dragged them out to a chopping block and hacked off their heads. They jammed these onto wooden posts, fixing the Archbishop's mitre in place by driving a nail right through his skull. Triumphantly, they set the heads above the gates of London Bridge.

The King had to take refuge in an unsafe outer part of the Tower. From here he sent a new request to the rebel leaders. He wanted them to meet him at Smithfield (a square within the walls of the city) and explain why they had not returned to their proper homes.

In fact most of the rebels had already set off home with their letters which contained the King's promises. 'Those who remained were extremists, politicians and criminals.' Despite this, Tyler felt he was

Executions taking place in the Tower

getting stronger all the time. He boasted that he could go where he pleased at the head of 20 000 men, and said that he would 'shave the beards' of all who opposed him. No wonder the King saw his priest before setting out, and rode to the meeting with armour hidden under his clothes.

Death and defeat

The fateful meeting at Smithfield took place on the afternoon of Saturday 15 June. When the King and his followers reached the square they formed up along the eastern side. Tyler's party 'arrayed themselves on the west side in great battles':

battles: battalions

> Tyler came to the King with great confidence, mounted on a little horse, that the commons might see him. He dismounted ... took the King by the hand, and shook his arm forcibly and roughly, saying to him, 'Brother, be of good cheer, for you shall have, in the fortnight that is to come, thanks from the commons even more than you have at the present hour....
>
>   Neither I nor my fellows will leave until we have got our charter just as we wish to have it, [with] certain points revised and added...'
>
> Anonimal Chronicle

Tyler added some vague threats. It seems that the King was equally vague, for the chronicles tell us he gave the rebel 'an easy answer'. Tyler, however, had worked himself into 'a great heat'. He called for some water and squirted it round inside his mouth in 'a very rude and disgusting fashion before the King's face'. The King's supporters were furious, and one cried out that Tyler was 'the greatest thief and robber in Kent':

> For these words Tyler tried to strike him with his dagger, and would have slain him in the King's presence, but the Mayor of London ... arrested him. And because he arrested him Tyler stabbed the Mayor with his dagger in the stomach in great wrath. But, as it pleased God, the Mayor was wearing armour (under his robes) and took no harm, but like a hardy and vigorous man he drew his sword and struck back at Tyler, and gave him a deep cut on the neck, and then a great cut on the head. And during this scuffle one of the King's followers drew his sword and ran Tyler two or three times through the body, mortally wounding him....
>
>   When the commons saw that their chieftain was dead ... they fell to the ground like beaten men, begging the King to forgive their misdeeds. The King was kind and merciful, and most of the rebels returned to their homes.
>
> Anonimal Chronicle

Questions

1 There were two or three signs that the meeting at Smithfield would be less friendly than the one at Mile End. Try to say what they were.

2 Look at the picture depicting Tyler's death. Try to identify two or three of the principal characters. Who appears twice? Try to suggest a possible reason.

3 One of the earlier reports of the meeting says that Tyler was fiddling with a dagger as he went up to the King. The writer seems to emphasise this. Why should he do so?

4 Look at both the extracts above. What is the writer's attitude to:–
   a) the King?
   b) the Mayor?
   c) Tyler?
   d) the rebels?

5 Look again at the picture. The artist has made one or two mistakes. Try to say what they are.

Death of Tyler *from Froissart's chronicle, showing Richard taking command of the rebels*

The final word

The Revolt had come to a sudden end. In one way the rebels had been defeated but in another way they had won a victory, for they had the King's letters promising nearly all they desired. This explains their readiness to return home quickly, leaving Tyler dead, and Ball and Straw as prisoners awaiting the hangman's rope.

Once the executions were over Richard issued a new lot of letters. These letters said that the previous ones had been obtained by force, and therefore counted for nothing. Serfs must still obey their masters!

The leaderless rebels could not strike back. They had snatched at freedom – freedom for themselves and the 'Commons' of England – but the King had outwitted them. His officials would no longer dare to press for the unpaid tax, but otherwise the Revolt was a failure. Freedom would come eventually, but only in a gradual way. The process took lifetimes rather than days.

Questions

1 In a few ways the old system lingers on, even today. Try to find out what a tied cottage is.
2 Look again at the rhyme about the Plague on page 20. Some people think it is really about the Peasants' Revolt. Weigh up this idea for yourself.
3 Pretend that you are a guard at the Tower of London In 1381. Write a diary describing what you see at the Tower – and from the Tower – between 12 June and 15 June. The map on page 37 will help you to imagine the different scenes.

INDEX